THE MA

BY NABU

THE POCKET ANUNNAKI DEVOTIONAL COMPANION OF THE MARDUKITES

Translations by Joshua Free

Originally published in 2010 as the Tablet-W Series of the Mardukite Research Organization in conjunction with Mardukite Truth Seeker Press

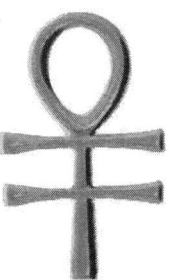

FIFTH ANNIVERSARY – THIRD EDITION
© 2015, Joshua Free

No part of this publication may be reproduced in any form or by any means, electronic or mechanical, including photocopying, recording, or by any information storage or retrieval system, without permission in writing from the publisher.

Also available in tri-lingual French Edition as:
LE LIVRE DE MARDUK PAR NABU

THE BOOK OF MARDUK
BY NABU

THE POCKET ANUNNAKI DEVOTIONAL
COMPANION OF THE MARDUKITES

**MARDUKITE
CHAMBERLAINS**

LOVINGLY DEDICATED TO:

MARDUK & SARPANIT
My Lord & Lady of Babylon
– who gave me life.

&

ANU – ENLIL – ENKI
The Spirit of the Supernal Trinity
– who gave us all life.

THE BOOK OF MARDUK BY NABU

ACKNOWLEDGMENTS

Cuneiform & Sigil Design by Joshua Free

Cuneiform Final Art by Jessica Brooks

Final Sigil & Cover Art by Sarah Banas

Transliteration & Translation by Joshua Free

WWW–MARDUKITE–COM

THE BOOK OF
MARDUK
BY NABU

TABLET OF CONTENTS

- Preface to the Third Edition ... 11
- Introduction & Application ... 13
- The Grand Invocation ... 16

THE SEVEN ANUNNAKI OF BABYLON
- Monday (*the Moon*) : Nanna-Sin ... 25
- Tuesday (*Mars*) : Nergal ... 31
- Wednesday (*Mercury*) : Nabu ... 37
- Thursday (*Jupiter*) : Marduk ... 43
- Friday (*Venus*) : Inanna-Ishtar ... 49
- Satuday (*Saturn*) : Ninurta ... 55
- Sunday (*the Sun*) : Samas-Utu ... 61

THE ANUNNAKI SUPERNAL TRINITY
- Enki (E.A.) : Neptune ... 69
- Enlil (EL) : System Command ... 75
- Anu (AN) : Uranus ... 81

PREFACE TO THE THIRD EDITION

Five years passed by since the *Book of Marduk by Nabu* started circulating privately among Mardukite Chamberlains. connected to the revolutionary discourse known as *Liber-50*, now available as my book, *Sumerian Religion*.

The *Book of Marduk by Nabu* reflects a very real modern philosophical and meta-spiritual movement that is connected specifically to the *Anunnaki* paradigm. In ancient Babylon, this was famously founded among the followers of **MARDUK** – recognized among the pantheon as the patron of Babylon city and the self-made *"King of the Gods"* for this *mythos*, with the assistance of the Nabu priesthood.

Many readers over the years misunderstood that *The Book of Marduk by Nabu* is not a transliteration of 'ancient' tablets. It is inspired by their language and style. Modern self-honest practitioners created this small volume to supplement a real system where communication with these specific 'alien intelligences' using is sought.

Work and development conducted by the *Mardukite Research Organization* from 2008 through 2012 is known as the '*Mardukite Core*' or else the

Necronomicon Anunnaki Legacy. The culmination of these materials and critical documents from the *Mardukite Truth Seeker Press* has reached the public in their entirety after having first been released privately to the *Mardukite Chamberlains.*

Mardukite Chamberlains made sweeping discoveries and revelations during the course of their active years. The question, particularly toward *Liber-50*, is 'how' this knowledge has been and can be accessed. The only suitable public answer is: *The Book of Marduk by Nabu.*

Within these pages a newcomer might glean the beauty of the system, but a more adept *seeker* of the mysteries will undoubtedly discover much more with little further suggestions and even less prompting. The resurrection of this *lost book* will most certainly be as well received now as it was <u>five years</u> ago, if not even more so today, as the work of the *Mardukite Research Organization* continues to reach new and wider audiences.

May the personal possession of this most treasured tome, bring you blessings as a talisman!

In Peace, Love & Unity – Always,

~ JOSHUA FREE
June 2015

INTRODUCTION and APPLICATION

We sealed seven gates – representative stations in Babylon. We allowed Each of the city-states to emphasize their own local patrons – a god and a goddess. We sought a unity for all existence of the gods, under the singular watchful eye of my father, MARDUK, son of ENKI.

Our father, ENKI, took MARDUK as apprentice to the magical and religious arts while in E.RIDU and I later took hold of these mysteries and dispersed the knowledge to my priest-scribes and magicians in Babylon – and in Egypt, where my family was recognized by other names.

Each of the "Seven" are embodiments of one of the seven gates forged in Babylon, homes to the gods of the "younger pantheon." It is true, the same seven-fold division may be found to fragment the *world of form* – corresponding to color, sound, or the ancient planets observed from Earth by our ancestors, seen as *"Guardians."*

The sevenfold planetary mystical paradigm is connected to the "Seven" of the Gates – and also correlate to an observable cycle of weekly time. Following the planet-ruling days offers the supplicant [or priest] an opportunity to meditate on a specific intention or ceremonial observation in the presence of (or to appeal to) each of the pair-bonded "sets" of *Anunnaki* "divine couples" honored in the "younger pantheon" of Babylon (as means of connecting with the representative affluent energetic current for each).

> Sunday – Sun – Shammash/Samas & Aya
> Monday – Moon – Nanna-Sin & Ningal
> Tuesday – Mars – Nergal & Ereshkigal
> Wednesday – Mercury – Nabu & Teshmet
> Thursday – Jupiter – Marduk & Sarpanit
> Friday – Venus – Ishtar/Inanna & Dumuzi
> Saturday – Saturn – Ninib/Ninurta & Ba'u

Within the domains of the "Seven" are all of the material and spiritual aspects that a priest-magician or supplicant seeks in life (e.g. ISHTAR for *love* or SAMAS for *truth*). One merely must appeal with self-honesty and true words to attain them. The original arts were set down in the ancient days – set down for men to remember us. Remember us, and we will remember you.

Our Names and the processions of the Gates are not there for the bedazzlement of the "occult initiate." There are very real metaphysical and spiritual lessons to be gleaned based on the division and fragmentation of the material universe – a mastery only attainable by a true and faithful relationship with the *Anunnaki* gods of your ancestors.

The spiritual power of the gods became subverted, altered and bastardized by humans into the myriad of mystical systems now available for your disposal, written by men with no better understanding of the energies they seek to invoke then those who read them. Some of these ancient traditions are falsely said to come from my hand.) The true priest-magician compels the power of the gods by friendship, trust, and honor; not through fear, threats and hatred.

By MARDUK, I learned the power of incantation he learned in Eridu. I was told to appease gods in his name, to speak the words of the higher.

MARDUK invoked the name of ENKI, our father, who, invoked the name of ANU. And so was born the magical "hierarchies" and correspondences that magicians have confused. I taught the magician-scribes of my order to invoke my name and seal during their petitions to the gods, in the Grand Invocation that I have given here, just as I learned it from MARDUK.

GRAND INVOCATION

ANU above me, King in Heaven.
ENLIL, Commander of the Airs.
ENKI, Lord of the Deep Earth.
I am NABU – hear my words..
I am the priest of MARDUK and SARPANIT.
Son of our father, ENKI and DAMKINA.
I am the priest in E.RIDU.
I am the magician in BABYLON.
My spell is the spell of ENKI.
My incantation is the incantation of MARDUK.
The Tablets of Destiny, I hold in my hands.
The Ankh of ANU and ANTU, I hold in my hands.
The wisdom of ENLIL and NINLIL, I call to me.
The Magic Circle of ENKI and DAMKINA,
   I conjure about me.
SHAMMASH and AYA are before me.
NANNA-SIN and NINGAL are behind me.
NERGAL and ERESHKIGAL are at my right side.
NINIB-NINURTA and BA'U are at my left side.
The blessed light of ISHTAR and DUMUZI
   shines favorably upon my sacred work.
It is not I, but MARDUK,
   who performs the incantations.

As should become increasingly apparent to the the contemporary folk of the current age, the *Anunnaki* are powerful and influential, though often directly unseen, forces behind the reality of the life you exist in – as your ancestors were well aware of. If you work with us in conjunction with the natural flow of the universal energies, then you will come face to face with your true destiny – *we will invite you home, again.*

Learn true-knowledge and overcome challenges of self-mastery in the physical. And then, dear *Seeker*, resolve to walk with us again among the stars, circumnavigating all the illusions placed before you in this world – have been raised before you as a test of your existence and strength of your '*astral body*'. When you truly prove yourself before us, we shall celebrate your arrival ...

                    NABU
                 21, June 2015 – Solstice

THE BOOK OF MARDUK
BY NABU

**MARDUKITE
CHAMBERLAINS**

THE SEVEN
ANUNNAKI
OF BABYLON

MONDAY
NANNA-SIN
THE MOON

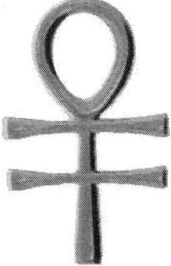

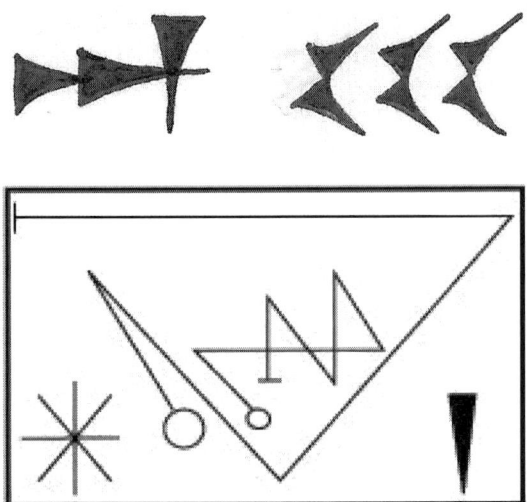

MONDAY – MOON – NANNA-SIN

To the ancients, the moon was the "sun at night." It illuminated the path for travelers and kept watch as the people slept. Just as the sun was invoked to grant judgments of the daytime, the moon is given the domain over the dreams of men. Being the first spiritual threshold (Gate) between earth and heaven, the moon is significantly linked to the astral plane. The priestesses (and later witches) of INANNA-ISHTAR revered the moon, called NANNA by Sumerians or Sin to the Babylonians, as their sky-father and/or spiritual-mate. ISHTAR literally was the "daughter of the moon" (and a twin to the sun/SAMAS) and her followers often also took this title.

Our pantheon places NANNA in the position of lunar god with the designation of 30, the basic lunar month of the Sumerian calendar (30 x 12 = 360). The name NANNA (or NANNAR) is actually an attribute of the full moon. He is called Sin (or SU.EN) when representing the crescent and the name for the new moon is: *AS.IM.BABBAR.* The lunar current is heavily water oriented with blue hues, though best represented ritually in the non-color spectrum (silver, black, white).

PRAYER TO NANNA & NINGAL

ilu-NANNA. ilu-SIN. ilu-istari-NINGAL.
ilu-NANNAR. ilu-NAMRASIT.
su-bu-u man-za-za ina ilani rabuti
  maru aplu ilu-ENLIL u ilu-NINLIL
nam-rat urru-ka ina sami-i ina sat musi
du natalu, nasaru anabu harranu-dim
u nisu ina bitu sat musi suttu
itti namrasit ina sami-i
kima diparu, kima ilu-SAMAS
samsatu ilu-NANNA namaru suttu
  agu
abu ilu-SAMAS
rimi-nin-ni-ma anaku ____ , apil ____ , sa
  ilu-sa ___ u ilu-istari-su ____ .
ilu-NANNA u ilu-NINGAL rimi-nin-
  ni-ma
kaparu anaku sillatu
  lu-us-tam-mar ilu-ut-ka
petu babu temu
li-iz-ziz ina imni-ya u sumuli-ya
  anaku arad-ka elu
an-un-na-ki ti-i-ru u
  na-an-za-zu

PRAYER TO NANNA & NINGAL

NANNA. SIN. NINGAL.
NANNAR. MOON.
Mighty One among the gods, son of ENLIL
  and NINLIL,
Brightest in the heavens at night,
Keeping watch, protecting weary travelers
And the people in their homes as they sleep.
Your brightness extends through the heavens,
Like a torch – Like a fire-god.
Radiance of NANNA, who reflects the
  dreams of men,
To you was born the SUN.
Be favorable to me, I, __ son of __ , whose
  god is __ and whose goddess is __ .
May NANNA and NINGAL deal graciously
  with me,
Cleanse me of iniquity that I may be free to
  call upon thee.
Open the Gates of your mysteries to me,
Stand on either side of me,
  a servant of the Highest.
May the ANUNNAKI come forth an be
  established.

**MARDUKITE
CHAMBERLAINS**

TUESDAY
NERGAL
MARS

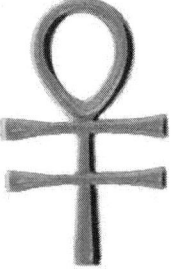

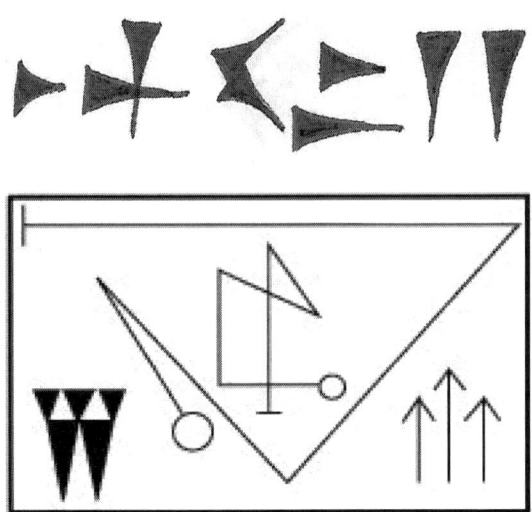

TUESDAY – MARS – NERGAL

The martian current has always been one of the most difficult to properly relay on a spiritual basis. To emphasize the primal fiery destruction would be all too simple. The current is best correlated to the Sumerian concept of *"Girra"* or *"fires of God."* The "hand" of God requires a representative vehicle in which to exercise even its own power in physical ways.

Underlying the power of Mars, and the demonstrator of this force in Babylon (NERGAL), is really "passion." The outer demonstrations of this pure attribute are what can later be deemed by men as lust, love, anger, jealousy and the like. But these are outer forms only – it is the passion, pure and true, that must be embraced. NERGAL is invoked, then, to temper the visions of anger or discord in our lives so we might embrace the passion beneath with clarity, which is anything but evil or destructive. The number of NERGAL is 8, showing that he is outside of the "heavenly" ranks (ending in 5 or 0). His abode is with ERESHKIGAL, who is Queen in the "Underworld." Combined, the pair represent the most "gothic," misunderstood and yet truly romantic elements and attributes of divinity and creation: passion and death.

PRAYER TO NERGAL & ERESHKIGAL

*ilu-NERGAL. ilu-IRRIGAL. Ilu-istari-
ERESHKIGAL. ilu-ERRA.
siru belu ersetu
ilu-istari-ERESHKIGAL, beltu ersetu
saqu-su manzazu
 it-ti ilani samu
ilu-NERGAL u ilu-istari-ERESHKIGAL
rimi-nin-ni-ma, ana-ku ___ , apil ____ ,
sa ilu-su ___ ilu-istar-su ___ .
banu-ya libbu alalu
di-ni uzzu ina ramanu libbu
ana-ku izuzzu mahru ze
petu babu temu
rimi-nin-ni-ma ina damu
 u du lemnutu seg ina ramanu zi
ana-ku arad-ka elu kamazu ze
 rimi-nin-ni-ma
babu-mah du pataru
an-un-na-ki ti-i-ru u
 na-an-za-zu*

PRAYER TO NERGAL & ERESHKIGAL

NERGAL. IRRIGAL. ERESHKIGAL.
ERRA. MARS.
Exalted Lord of the Underworld.
ERESHKIGAL, Queen of the Underworld.
Great is your place
  among the gods of heaven.
NERGAL and ERESHKIGAL,
Truly have mercy on me, __ , son of ___ ,
  whose god is ___ , whose goddess is ___ .
May your hearts be tempered.
Temper also the anger within my heart,
That I may stand before you,
Make me perfect to call upon you,
Open the Gates of your understanding to me.
Grant me a favorable death
  and keep evil from me in life.
I, a servant of the Highest, kneel before thee,
  take pity on me.
May the Great Doors stand open.
May the ANUNNAKI return and
  be established.

**MARDUKITE
CHAMBERLAINS**

WEDNESDAY
NABU
MERCURY

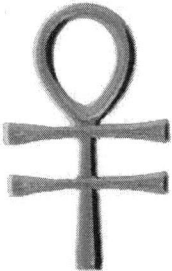

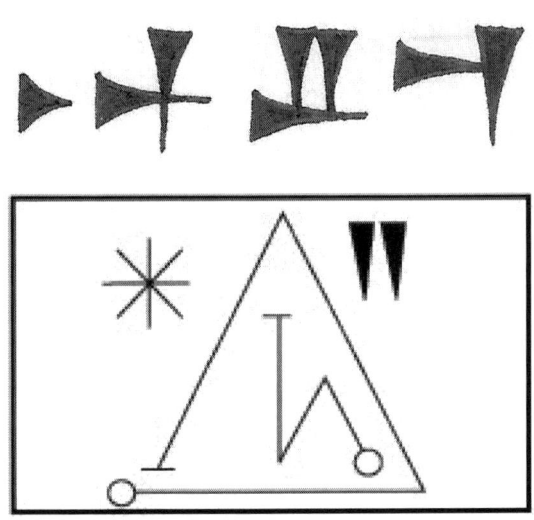

WEDNESDAY – MERCURY – NABU

The *Mercurial* current is connected to divination: relaying information through the universe, or else, communication. Whether it is prayers, a song, the recording of history or the prediction of the future, the performance is undertaken by the blessing of the "scribe-messenger" of the gods. *"Thoth"* or *"Hermes"* is sometimes identified for this current, demonstrating the connection to magic systems, occultism and the air element. Babylonian tradition observes me, NABU, as son of MARDUK, as the scribe-priest of the gods, the keeper of the "destinies" among the younger pantheon with the designation of 12 (connecting heavenly-time and earth-time).

My scribe-priests worked diligently during the Babylonian era forging tablet texts based on the Sumerian tradition, supporting our local patron, MARDUK, as *King of the Gods*, usurping the position of ENLIL and usurping the rights of the position by NINURTA for both spiritual and physical politics. This travesty in Babylon that we conducted, but which is being currently resolved, shows the power of knowledge, true or false, and how it can be used to shape people and the world. Invoke my name for clarity and discernment in the seeking of truth. My color is blue.

PRAYER TO NABU & TESHMET

ilu-NABU. ilu-TUTU. ilu-istari-TESHMET
  ilu-istari-TASMIT. ilu-NEBOS.
tupsarru si-mat ilani
sarru nam-zu si-mat ilani
asaridu bukur ilu-MARDUK u ilu-
  SARPANIT
ilu-NABU na-as duppu si-mat
  ilani
ramanu ur-hi suttu
  lid-mi-ik
ilu-NABU u ilu-TASMITU
  ka-ba-a si-ma-a suk-na ya-si-sa
rimi-nin-ni-ma, ana-ku ___ , apil ___ sa
  ilu-sa ___ u ilu-istari-su ___ .
ebbu ramanu nam-eme-sig u ummuqu
  si-mi-i su-pi-ya
petu babu temu
amat a-kab-bu-u kima a-kab-bu-u
  lu-u ma-ag-rat
sumu-ka ka-lis ina pi nisi ta-a-ab
anaku arad-ka elu
an-un-na-ki ti-i-ru u
  na-an-za-zu

PRAYER TO NABU & TESHMET

NABU. TUTU. TESHMET – TASMIT(U).
NEBOS. MERCURIOS.
Scribe among the Gods,
Keeper of the Wisdom of the Gods,
Firstborn of MARDUK and SARPANIT.
NABU, Bearer of the Tablet of Destinies
  of the gods,
May my dreams [destiny] be filled with
  prosperity.
May my petitions fall on the ears of
  NABU & TASMIT.
Be favorable to me, I, __ son of __ , whose
  god is __ and whose goddess is __ .
Cleanse me of false knowledge, that I might
  be ft to call upon thee.
Open the Gates of your understanding to me.
Bless my mouth with true words to speak
  the prayers.
May the prayers rise from the lips of the
  people.
I am a servant of the Highest,
May the ANUNNAKI come forth and be
  established.

**MARDUKITE
CHAMBERLAINS**

THURSDAY
MARDUK
JUPITER

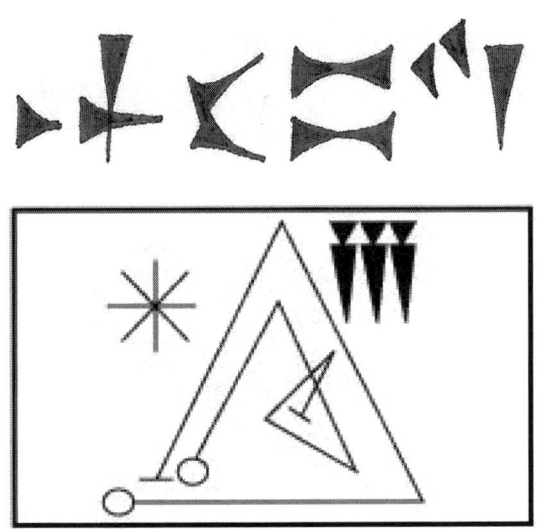

THURSDAY – JUPITER – MARDUK

The industrious and raw expansive power of Jupiter is placed at the height of most 'Olympian' pantheons (*Zeus* or similar). "Jupiter" comes from the Romans: *Dys Pater*, meaning "Father-God." This energetic current commands outright worldly success as and the magic of spirits: command of the hierarchies. Elder Gods originally attributed this position to ENLIL in Sumer. I personally heralded my father, MARDUK, into Enlilship of the "younger pantheon" in Babylon. Our tradition there, and in Egypt, was wholly based on him being the centralized figure. Invoke my father for his strength and power, as well as a petitioner to the Elder Gods.

He is exalted as the Master of Magicians, carrying the mysteries of my grandfather, ENKI, to Babylon, and bestowing the traditions upon me to relay. The original designation of Jupiter is 50, the number attributed first to ENLIL and later to MARDUK by the Babylonians, who first was given the number 10. The color of the current is purple, but also airy and fiery colors (yellow, orange, black). This energy is preferred by many leaders and law enforcing folk, lending to those who are pure to receive it, the power to command the material world.

PRAYER TO MARDUK & SARPANIT

ilu-MAR.DUG. ilu-MAR.DUK. ilu-istari-
  ZARPANIT. ilu-silik-MULU.KHI DIL.GAN.
lugal arali, belu asipu
ilu-su BAB.ILI
ilu-SARPANIT(UM), belitu istari-su BAB.ILI
gasru u sapsu ina an-ki
  zi atwu
belu u belitu su BAB.ILI
maharu ramanu arua abnu-gesnu, abnu-
  uqnu u hurasu
dinu-ma ramanu lid-mi-ik
anaku ___ apil ___ sa ilu-su ___ u
  ilu-istar-su ___ .
lu-us-tam-mar ilu-ut-ka
  u atwu ramanu maharu karabu
petu babu temu – petu babu idu
ina ki-bi-ti-ka sir-ti lu-ub-lut lu-us-lim-ma
napsiti narbu ramanu ki-bi su
  su-sud ilani samu
anaku arad-ka elu
an-un-na-ki ti-i-ru u
  na-an-za-zu

PRAYER TO MARDUK & SARPANIT

MARDUK. MERODACH. SARPANIT.
MULU-KHI. JUPITER.
Lord of the Lands, Master of Magicians,
God of Babylon.
SARPANIT, Lady of Babylon.
Mighty and powerful on earth and heaven
  are your words.
Lord and Lady of Babylon,
Accept my offerings of alabaster, lapis lazuli
  and gold.
Judge my life favorably,
I ___ , son of ____ , whose god is ____ , and
  whose goddess is ____ .
Make me fit to behold your divinity
  and teach me to receive thy blessings.
Open the Gates of your power to me.
Let me live. Let me be perfect.
Command greatness in my life as your
  expansion permeates the gods of heaven.
I am a servant of the Highest.
May the ANUNNAKI come forth and
  be established.

**MARDUKITE
CHAMBERLAINS**

FRIDAY
ISHTAR
VENUS

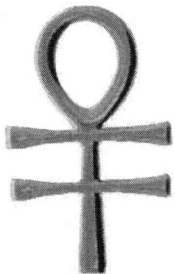

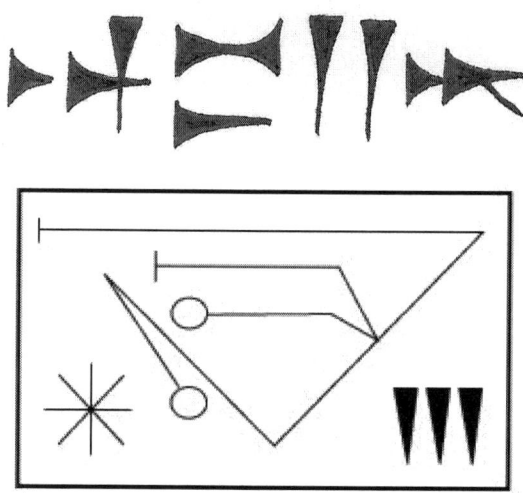

FRIDAY – VENUS – ISHTAR

Most famous among energetic currents of these mysteries is Venusian. It is always dedicated to the "goddess of love and war." A determined goddess, she made her place among all ancient pantheons: whether *Isis, Aphrodite, Ashtoreth...* she is also known as the "goddess of witches," and celebrated in their rites. In Babylon, by request of MARDUK, her political anger was appeased by being established as ISHTAR (Venus).

When ISHTAR and MARDUK were not pair-bonded (as intended), each took it upon themselves to elevate and usurp their own positions among our "younger pantheon."

The Venusian current (and that of Jupiter) are extremely powerful and actively raw energies. They are not always as obvious with their executions, such as you might find with the Sun or Mars, but they store mass amounts of energy for eventual release at the most "propitious" or favorable times. ISHTAR may be invoked to channel energies directed toward the acquisition of desires. (A wise one will be certain this is for their higher good first.) Her number is 15. Colors are green, yellow-green and white, and her elements are water and earth.

PRAYER TO ISHTAR & DUMUZI

ilu-INANNA. ilu-istari-ISHTAR. ilu-
DUMUZI. ilu-ISTAR.
belitu, martu-su ilu-NANNA-SIN
  sa karabu ina samu
ramu-su ilu-ANU, rabianu samu
namru-sat musi
lu-dub-gar-ra sat musi
li-iz-ziz ilu-istari-ya ina sumili-ya
  sutlumu karabu nissanu sabu u ilani
ilu-istari-ISHTAR u ilu-DUMUZI
rimi-nin-ni-ma, ana-ku ___ apil ___ sa
  ilu-sa ___ u ilu-istar-su ___
mesu-ya nigussu, anaku aga
  simtu maharu zi qistu
petu babu temu
li-iz-ziz ramanu manahtu-su zid
a-mat a-kab-bu-u kima a-kab-bu-u lu-u
  ma-ag-rat
is-ti-' nam-ri-ir-ri-ki lim-mi-ru samu
  kima nasaru sabu-su karabu
si-lim itti ya-a-tu-u anaku arad-ka elu
an-un-na-ki ti-i-ru u
  na-an-za-zu

PRAYER TO ISHTAR & DUMUZI

INANNA. ISHTAR. DUMUZI.
ISTARI VENUS.
Queen, Daughter of the Moon,
  who is blessed by the heavens,
Beloved of ANU, Command in Heaven,
Brightness of the Evening,
Huntress of the Night,
Do come to stand favorably at my side,
  grant me the fruits of men and gods.
ISHTAR and DUMUZI,
Be favorable to me, I, ___ son of ___ , whose
  god is ___ and whose goddess is ___ ,
Cleanse me of impurity make me a vessel
  fit to receive your rewards.
Open the Gates of your understanding to me.
May my actions be true.
May the words I speak bring me to success.
May your light shinning in the heavens
  be a guide to all men you bless favorably.
Bless me, a servant of the Highest.
May the ANUNNAKI come forth and
  be established.

**MARDUKITE
CHAMBERLAINS**

SATURDAY
NINURTA
SATURN

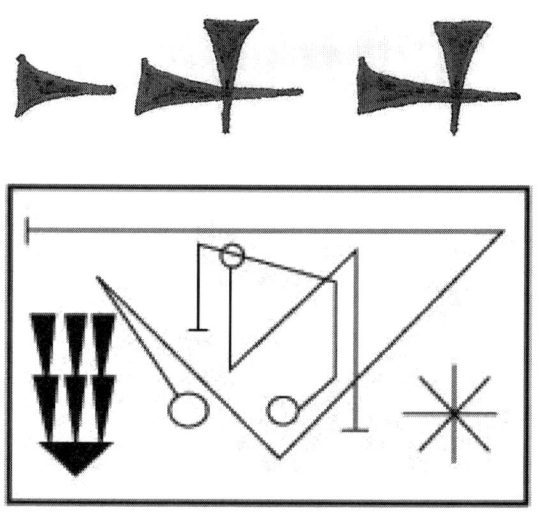

SATURDAY – SATURN – NINURTA

Among planets, Saturn is traditionally dark and secretive, representing hidden power and the *"hidden key"* by which one may be released from the material world of Gates and illusions.

The Saturnalian current is a threshold to the Outer Ones that the secret societies and mystery schools have covertly sought through the ages. NINURTA represents Saturn in Mesopotamia. He also reflects the dark secret of Babylon: He is the heir to Enlilship, a position MARDUK usurped.

In the Babylonian system, NINURTA is given a designation of 4. This indicates he is outside of the 'Olympian pantheon' of 'sky gods,' waiting to take his place, being heir of ENLIL with the number 50. Saturn energy is just as passively introspective as it is actively reflecting the outer world. These lessons demand confronting dark, repressed, guilt-laden aspects of themselves to ascend to self-honest wholeness. The elements of *air* and *earth* are both present in this current and the darker color spectrum is most resonant. Invoke NINURTA to aid in one's own path toward mastery in addition to giving recognition to correct the aspects that have kept the very system from achieving its own wholeness.

PRAYER TO NINURTA & BA'U

ilu-NINURTA. ilu-NINIB. ilu-istari-BA'U.
 ilu-ADAR.
siptu aplu gas-ru bukur ilu-ENLIL
su-bu-u man-za-za ina ilani rabuti
 siru rubu-su ilu-ENLIL u ilu-NINMAH
belu u beltu sihip same u erseti
ilu-NINIB u ilu-istari-BA'U
atwu karabu-ya kisalmahu
ana-ku ___ apil ___ sa ilu-su ___ u
 ilu-istar-su ___
an-ni pu-tur
sir-ti pu-sur
lu-us-tam-mar ilu-ut-ka
 u atwu ramanu lid-mi-ik
petu babu temu,
 anaku arad-ka elu
ilu-istar-BA'U, biltu sur-bu-tu, sela ummu
ilu-NINIB, nisirtu qarradu ilu-ENLIL
ki-bit narbu ramanu zi
si-lim itti ya-a-tu-u
sumu-ka ka-lis ina pi nisi
 ta-a-ab
an-un-na-ki ti-i-ru u
 na-an-za-zu

PRAYER TO NINURTA & BA'U

NINURTA. NINIB. BA'U.
ADAR. SATURN.
Mighty firstborn son of ENLIL.
Great is your place among the gods,
  royal prince of ENLIL and NINMAH.
Lord and Lady of the heavenly abode,
NINIB and BA'U,
Speak favorably of me in your courts,
I, ___ , son of ___ , whose god is ____ , and
  whose goddess is ____ .
Absolve me of my sins.
Remove my iniquities.
Make me fit to call upon and receive your
  blessings.
Open the Gates of you Understanding to me,
  a servant of the Highest,
BA'U, Mighty Lady, merciful mother.
NINIB, hidden warrior of ENLIL.
Command greatness in my life.
Look upon me favorably.
May your name be in the mouth of the
  people.
May the ANUNNAKI return and
  be established.

**MARDUKITE
CHAMBERLAINS**

SUNDAY
SHAMMASH
THE SUN

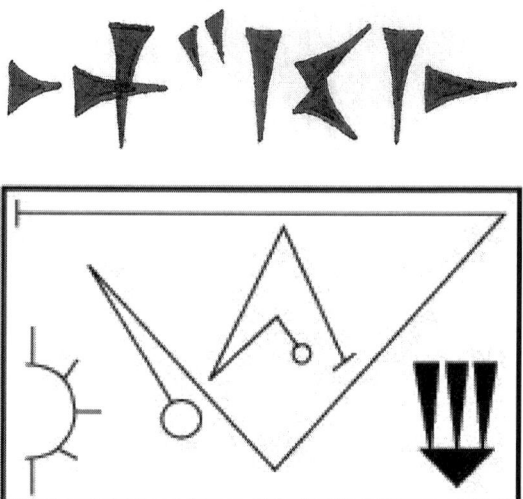

SUNDAY – SUN – SHAMMASH

The sun represents the brilliance and radiance of life on earth. It is the light that allows organic life to grow and it is also the manner in which time is divided, including a lifespan. The sun also symbolizes expansive powerful energy and is often invoked for general success and well-being in this existence (and the next). The fiery nature of the star is called to "incinerate iniquities" and also to reveal darkness or lies: the revelation of truth. Mistaken as monotheistic solar worship, the veneration of the sun is the celebration of life, and so annual festivals were marked by the path of the sun (at solstices and equinoxes). As a representative of "Heaven," the sun signifies the physical presence and watchful eye of "God" and is invoked to bring righteous judgment to critical situations.

In the Babylonian pantheon, the solar designation of 20 is given to SAMAS (*Shammash*) also known by the Sumerians as UTU. The colors of this energy current are bright (yellow, white, gold) and the dominant element is clearly fire or *starfire*. The prayer that follows, invokes SAMAS to come forth and be established as the supreme judge of the destinies of men on earth.

PRAYER TO SHAMMASH & AYA

ilu-SHAMMASH. ilu-UTU. ilu-istari-AYA.
ilu-SAMAS. samsu.
anqullu u igigallu
dinu ilani
maru aplu ilu-NANNA-SIN
sapiru nam-simtu apitu
ilu-SAMAS u ilu-AYA
karabu danu simtu
metequ damaqu
la-kasadu immu kararu
ilu-SAMAS u ilu-AYA
si-lim itti ya-a-tu-u ___ , apil ___ ,
* sa ilu-sa ___ , ilu-istar-su ___ .*
napahu ramanu sir-tu
lu-ub-lut lu-us-lim-ma maharu nuru
enu atwu uznu ilu-ENLIL
petu babu temu
sumu-ka ka-lis ina pi nisi ta-a-ab
qibitu nig-silim ina ramanu
* napistu*
ana-ku arad-ka elu
an-un-na-ki ti-i-ru u
* na-an-za-zu.*

PRAYER TO SHAMMASH & AYA

SHAMMASH. UTU. AYA.
SAMAS. SUN.
Fiery and Powerful One,
Judge among the gods,
Son of the Moon-god,
Overseer of the destinies of the lands.
SHAMMASH and AYA,
Be the favorable judges of my destiny.
May the path be prosperous.
Unequaled light of day,
SHAMMASH and AYA
Shine favorably on me, __ , son of __ ,
  whose god is __ and whose goddess is __ .
Incinerate my iniquities.
Make me perfect to behold your light.
Lord, who appeals to the ears of ENLIL,
Open the Gates of your understanding to me.
Permanent is your mighty word on earth.
May your unquestioned command dictate
  prosperity in my life.
I am a servant of the Highest,
May the ANUNNAKI return and
  be established.

**MARDUKITE
CHAMBERLAINS**

THE SUPERNAL ANUNNAKI OF THE TRINITY

ENKI
E.A.
(NEPTUNE)

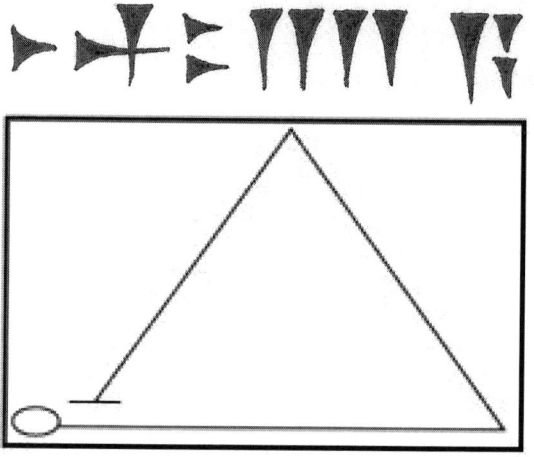

ENKI

ENKI assisted his brother ENLIL in developing the local universe, pre-Babylonian Sumer, and the organization of the physical world. Later, ENKI or E.A. ("Whose House is Water") is given domain over physical manifestation and creation in the form of "magic." In Babylon we gave to him the name of EN.KI meaning "Lord of the Earth." In raising him to this position among the people it was much easier for his son, MARDUK, to be given a high station as well.

The elements *earth* and *air* are strong in this energetic current. ENKI is sometimes referred to as "Our Father" among *our* Race of Marduk. He is given charge of the *"Word of Power"* [called MAAT by the Egyptians] that charges the incantations of magic that breathe changes into the universe. These secrets were passed onto MARDUK and myself. They became the foundation of our traditions in Babylon and Egypt. As a planetary power, ENKI is Neptune, the Greek 'Poseidon of the Deep.' His power is ancient and strong knowing no boundaries in the universe. For a time he had in his possession the Anunnaki *Tablets of Destiny* - the 'Arts of Civilization' powering the magic of the priests in Babylon.

PRAYER TO ENKI & DAMKINA

ilu-E.A ilu-IA ilu-EN.KI
ilu-istari-NIN.KI ilu-istari-DAM.KI.NA
ilu-EN.KI samu-ya sa mesari eresti
ilu-istari-DAM.KI.NA sar-rat kal
  an-un-na-ki ilani la-tu
ilu-EN.KI u ilu-istari-DAM.KI.NA
  sur-ba-ti ina ilani
  la-u parsuki
rimi-nin-ni-ma anaku ___ apil ___ sa
  ilu-sa ___ u ilu-istari-sa ___
abu u ummu kispu
nabatu kabasu ramanu manahtu
rasanu-ya rigmu ina ramanu siptu
ki-bi-ma lis-si-mi zik-ri
amat a-kab-bu-u kima a-kab-bu-u
  lu-u ma-ag-rat
dinu-ma ramanu lid-mi-ik
lu-us-tam-mar ilu-ut-ka nabatu anaku
  arad-ka elu
an-un-na-ki ti-i-ru u
  na-an-za-zu
u emedu salimu menu u tes
  enu zid katamu [AN.KI] sihip
  same u eresti

PRAYER TO ENKI & DAMKINA

EA. IA. ENKI.
NINKI. DAMKINA.
ENKI, Your name is the depths of the Earth.
DAMKINA, Queen among the Anunnaki
  Gods
ENKI and DAMKINA,
  You are great among the gods,
  Mighty is your command.
Be favorable to me ___ son of ___ whose
  god is ___ and whose goddess is ___ .
Father and Mother of Magic,
Shine upon my work.
Be the voice of my incantations.
Speak and let the Word by heard.
Let the Word I speak, when I speak it,
  be favorable.
Open the Gates of your understanding.
Judge my existence favorably.
Let your Divine Light shine through me,
  a servant of the Highest.
May the Anunnaki come forth and
  be established.
And may peace, love and unity,
  reign true throughout the Universe.

ENLIL
EL
(EARTH)

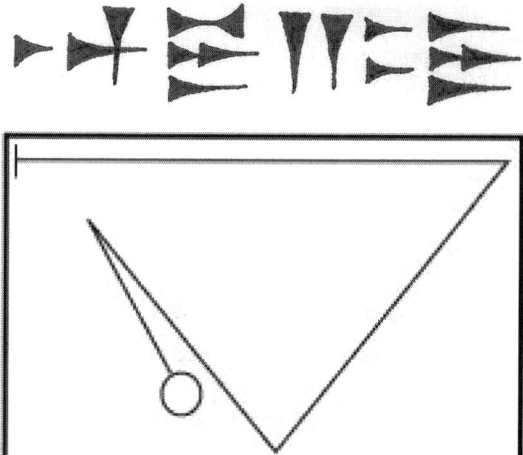

ENLIL

ENLIL is "Lord of the Command" – heir to *Anuship* in 'Heaven', position of 'God' in the local universe. This shift in power began the Judeo-Semitic age, when ENLIL appeared to the people of the "Holy Lands" as "Jehovah." It can be said that ENLIL is indeed the God of the Israelites and the Judeo-Christian and Islamic traditions.

Duality split the pantheon between lineages of ENLIL and ENKI occurred on Earth and in Heaven. ENLIL should be rightfully acknowledged as the power of *Anuship* in modern times, with his own heir, NINURTA as successor. Such was the original arrangement for the last age and for the "peace, love and unity to reign true in the Universe," it is essential that the perceptions of these traditions, in addition to their realizations in modern times, is carried in self-honesty.

Jupiter is the original current of ENLIL, though we observe MARDUK in Babylon, and the power to execute "*Anuship*" in the material world – an exercise of power in elemental domains of *air* and *fire* elements. Where ENKI is "Lord of the Earth," ENLIL is seen as "Lord of the Airs," the intermediary space bonding (between) the earth and the heavens.

PRAYER TO ENLIL & NINLIL

ilu-ENLIL ilu-BEL
ilu-istari-NINLIL ilu-istari-BELTU
sumu-ya sa dug-ga
rigmu-ya dug-ga samu u erseti
ilu-ENLIL abu ilani
ilu-BEL-ENLIL u ilu-istari-
  BELITU-NINLIL
zi kima ramanu abu u ummu anaku ___
  apil ___ *sa ilu-su* ___
  ilu-istari-su ___
ka-ba-a sutlumu ramanu tehu
  u amaru dingir-ya itti ilani
sutlumu-lu manzazu-ya itti ilani masu
banu anaku aga zaku temu
petu babu temu
karabu ramanu manahtu
  u zaqtu napharu
lu-us-tam-mar ilu-ut-ka nabatu anaku
  arad-ka elu
qibitu narbu ina [An.Ki] sihip same u eresti
an-un-na-ki ti-i-ru u
  na-an-za-zu
u emedu salimu menu u tes
  enu zid katamu [An.Ki] sihip same u eresti

PRAYER TO ENLIL & NINLIL

ENLIL. BEL.
NINLIL. BELTU.
Your name is the command.
Your voice rules the Heavens and Earth.
ENLIL, Father of the Gods,
BEL-ENLIL and BELITU-NINLIL,
You are as a father and mother to me ___ ,
  son of ___ , whose god is ____ and whose
  goddess is ____ .
At your command, allow me to approach
  and behold your divinity among the gods.
Let not your place among the gods
  be forgotten.
Make me a vessel of clear understanding.
Open the Gates of your understanding to me.
Bless me in my workings
  and show me wholeness.
Let your divine light shine through me,
  a servant of the Highest.
Command greatness in the Universe.
May the Anunnaki come forth and
  be established,
 And may peace, love and unity
   reign true throughout the Universe.

ANU
AN
(URANUS)

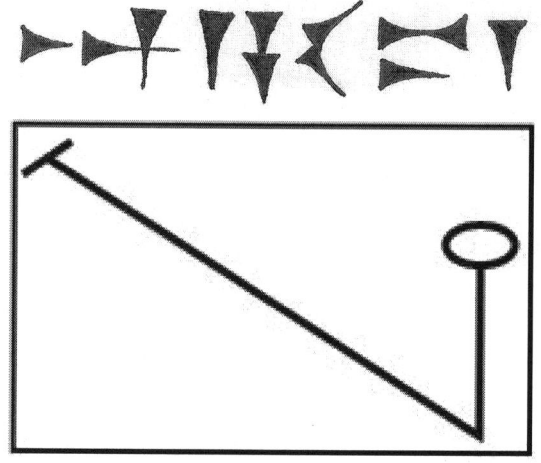

ANU

From the start of recorded history in Sumer, cuneiform tablets kept by NABU *priest-scribes* , it is ANU who is given role of "Father in Heaven," All-Father of the gods. This is what He was to us all, the father of both ENLIL and ENKI. All members of the Anunnaki pantheon from both lineages are His children.

The *"House of Anu"* is the "domain of Heaven," also the name given to the planet Uranus [UR-ANU]. His heavenly force has not always been immediately felt on earth, and has instead, been left to his heirs, ENLIL and ENKI, to command the cosmos in his stead.

ANU, the blessed Father of us all, shall ever remain in the mouth of the people – in the prayers. His legacy shall always remain on epic tablets and through the deeds of his children. His place in Heaven shall always be known to us, though it will be filled by another, as ANU has left us now with only his Shade remaining – and a position in the heavens meant to be filled by ENLIL (and his successor, NINURTA). With the dawning of the New Age comes another change in divinity. Let self-honest peace, love and unity reign true through the Universe when it does.

PRAYER TO ANU & ANTU

ilu-ANU ilu-AN ilu-AN.NA
ilu-istari-AN.TU
ilu-ANU abu ina samu
ilu-AN.NA samu-sa zi nigul sumu
daru-sa zi gitmalu-ya amatu
duru-sa zi dingir-ya edullu
zi biritu [an.sar] samu u [ki.sar] erseti
  sa-zi u'uru
madu ilani
  duru risatu zi mulammu
guhsu-ya gistaggu
  la urru
ilu-istaru-AN.TU ummu samu u nabalu
si-lim itti-ya a-tu-u
dingir hamdan ina samu lu-us-tam-mar
  itu-ut-ka u atwu ramanu lid-mi-ik
anaku ___ apil ___ sa ilu-su ___
  ilu-istar-su ___
anaku izuzzu wasru gudmu zi
anaku arad-ka-ya
  arad-ka elu
an-un-na-ki ahurru-ya
  ti-i-ru u na-an-za-zu

PRAYER TO ANU & ANTU

ANU. AN. ANNA.
ANTU.
ANU, Father in Heaven.
Heaven is your everlasting name.
Eternal is your perfect Word.
Forever is your Divine Kingdom.
The domain of Heaven and Earth
  is yours to command.
May the Great Gods
  ever rejoice in your splendor.
May your Altar of Offering
  never be empty.
ANTU, Mother of the Sky and Land,
Be favorable to me.
Divine Union of Heaven, make me fit
  to call upon and receive your blessings.
I, son of ___ whose god is ___ and whose
  goddess is ___ ,
Stand humbly before thee in praise.
I am thy servant –
  a servant of the Highest.
May the Anunnaki, your children,
  come forth and be established.

Would you like to know more???

**ENTER THE REALM
OF THE**

**MARDUKITE
CHAMBERLAINS**

NECRONOMICON ANUNNAKI BIBLE
Edited by Joshua Free

The Necronomicon - a masterpiece of Mesopotamian Mardukite Magic, Mysticism and primordial spirituality! This definitive edition contains the complete Year 1 tablet cycle from the "Mardukite Chamberlains" including Liber N – *Necronomicon*, Liber LL – *Liturgy & Lore*, Liber GG – *Gatekeepers Grimoire* and the coveted Liber 9. These are the raw underground materials have shaped the existence of man's beliefs and practices for thousands of years – right from the heart of Sumer, Babylon and Egypt! A Mardukite compendium of intensive historical, spiritual and mystical research drawn from very real and researchable tablets... enough to support a very real *"Necronomicon"* Anunnaki revival tradition! Join hundreds of others who have enjoyed the best of what the next generation has to offer. What has come before is but a shadow to the realizations now capable to all self-honest Truth Seekers! Rediscover the most ancient records of magic and mysticism – the most ancient traditions of Gods and Men lay here waiting to be unveiled!

THE BOOK OF ELVEN-FAERIE
by Joshua Free

The original underground masterpiece *comes alive* and in print available to the public for the *first time ever!* Follow the ancient traditions of Mesopotamia as they evolve into the systems of Western Europe. Discover how the most arcane practices actually shaped the beliefs of the western world and learn how mystical lineages of modern "folk magic" can be actually traced through the evolution of human civilization on the planet – all the way back to the ancient Anunnaki traditions of Sumerians, Babylonians, Egyptians, etc. and becoming the practices of the Tuatha de Dannan (Tuatha d'Anu) and other Celtic tribes. Ever popular in the underground, this book includes the complete *Book of Elven-Faerie* discourse with its corresponding "Grimoires" of Elven-Faerie traditions and forest magick, bring a complete Elvish Tradition to light for the first time in printed history. This book restores the historical basis of the modern "New Age" movements resulting from one Seeker's pursuits into the origins of the "Druids."

SUMERIAN RELIGION
by Joshua Free

The most critically acclaimed materials from the Mardukites: an account of the evolution of the Sumerian Tradition (into Babylonian, etc.) such as the modern world has never before had access to, developed by the next generation of seekers actively using this revival tradition in present day – not merely the presentation of dry academic renderings of obscure tablets: *Sumerian Religion* will take you on a progressive journey that is just as relevant and critical today as it was thousands of years ago – *if not more so.* *Sumerian Religion* is the perfect practical companion to *all systems and traditions* as it displays the origins of human traditions on the planet, something which all can relate to. As unique as it is practical – supporting a revival tradition revealing the nature, origins and traditions connected to the "Star-Gates" of the *Anunnaki Alien Gods of Mesopotamia*, which the public contemporary society has previously only known through nearly insubstantial renderings. A clearly understood volume offering a revolutionary perspective towards understanding Life, the Universe & Everything! [*These materials also known as Gates of the Necronomicon.*]

JOSHUA FREE

Developed by the Mardukite Research Organization

Made in the USA
Middletown, DE
19 July 2025